Amelia Boman

Chai Masala Cupcakes

PISTACHIO AND ROSE-WATER CUPCAKES

(Makes 12)

These delicate little delights capture the essence of the Middle East in the form the quintessential tea-time classic, cupcakes. Rose and pistachio flavours filtered into north India with the Mughal Empire in the sixteenth century and have since become staple components of Indian cuisine, especially desserts. Roasted pistachio nuts create a pungent flavour in these cupcakes, which is complemented by the delicately fragrant rose-water icing.

Ingredients

50 g shelled pistachios
(plus extra as desired for decorating)
120 ml plain yoghurt
160 ml milk
75 ml vegetable oil
150 g caster sugar
100 g plain flour
2 tbsp corn flour
½ tsp baking powder
½ tsp bicarbonate of soda
¼ tsp salt
1 tsp ground cardamom

For the Icing

300 ml crème fraîche
40 g icing sugar
2 tbsp rose water
a drop of pink food colouring if desired.

Method

* Preheat oven to gas mark 4/180°C/350°F.
* Line a 12-cavity cupcake tin with cases.
* Place the pistachio nuts in a frying pan and dry roast over a medium heat until vividly green and fragrant.
* Remove from the heat and allow to cool.
* In a large mixing bowl, whisk together the yoghurt, milk, oil, and sugar until smooth and well combined.
* Sift in the flour, corn flour, baking powder, baking soda, and salt; and beat to create a smooth batter.
* Roughly chop the cooled pistachio nuts, and fold into the batter along with the cardamom.
* Divide the batter equally among the 12 muffin cases. They should be about two thirds full.
* Bake for 25 minutes until lightly golden and springy to the touch.
* Transfer to a wire rack to cool while you prepare the icing.
* Whip together the crème fraîche, icing sugar, rose water, and food colouring (if using) until well combined.
* Keep the icing refrigerated until just before serving. When the cupcakes are completely cool and you are ready to serve them, swirl some icing on top of each cake and sprinkle with extra roasted pistachio nuts if desired.

Pistachio and Rose-Water Cupcakes

INDIAN-INSPIRED CARROT-CAKE LOAF

(Serves 6)

Carrots have been one of Jay's favourite foods since he was a toddler. Now he likes them transformed into a carrot cake. This recipe combines a traditional carrot cake with flavours from an Indian carrot pudding (Gajar ka Halwa, page 64) to produce an incredibly moist, very pleasing fusion loaf—a great twist for all carrot cake lovers.

Ingredients

200 g caster sugar
40 g dark muscovado sugar (or add an extra 50 g caster sugar)
120 ml vegetable oil
180 ml plain thick-set yoghurt
200 g plain flour
1½ tsp bicarbonate of soda
½ tsp baking powder
½ tsp salt
1½ tsp cinnamon
¾ tsp ground ginger
½ tsp grated nutmeg
½ tsp ground cardamom
240 g finely grated carrot
2 tbsp chopped shelled pistachio nuts

Method

* Preheat oven to gas mark 4/350°C/175°F.
* Grease and line the inside of a 23 x 12.5 cm loaf tin.
* Combine the sugar, vegetable oil, and yoghurt in a large mixing bowl and whisk until smooth.
* Sift in the flour, bicarbonate of soda, baking powder, salt, cinnamon, and ginger; and beat to create a smooth, well-mixed cake batter.
* Add the nutmeg, cardamom, and carrots and fold the mixture together.
* Pour the mixture into the prepared loaf tin and scatter the pistachio nuts over the top.
* Bake in the middle of the oven for 55–60 minutes or until a skewer put into the middle of the loaf comes out clean.
* Allow to cool in the tin on a wire rack for 15 minutes before turning out of the tin and allowing to cool completely.
* Cut into slices and serve. For that little extra touch—cut into thick slices (about 1.5 to 2 cm thick) and grill on one side until nicely toasted. Spread with cream cheese and serve warm.

Indian Inspired Carrotcake Loaf

BAKLAVA PANCAKE CAKE

(Serves 4–6)

Baklava is a signature Middle Eastern dessert; however, the flavours of pistachio and rose water are reflected throughout Indian cuisine, especially by a pretty little sweet named "Phool Khaja," one of Mum's favourite sweets. The Indian equivalent to baklava, it is made in the same way by layering flaky pastry with nuts and floral essences and then soaking the baked pastry in sugar syrup. This lighter, easier version made by layering crepes makes a stunning yet simple summer dessert and can be made just as easily in a frying pan over a barbecue.

For the Pancakes
200 g plain flour
1 tsp baking powder
1/4 tsp salt
25 g butter (melted)
400 ml milk (cold)

For the Honey Syrup
80 ml water
85 g honey
50 g caster sugar
1/2 tsp rose water
1/4 tsp ground cardamom
a few strands of saffron
25 g shelled pistachios

Method
* Start by preheating oven to gas mark 4/180°C/350°F.
* Now place the pistachios in a 15-cm frying pan and dry roast over a medium heat until aromatic. You will notice that they turn a much more vivid green.
* Transfer the nuts to a plate to cool and rinse out the pan. Dry thoroughly and set over a medium-high heat.
* Prepare the pancake batter by sifting the flour, baking powder, and salt into a mixing bowl.
* Pour in the butter, followed by the milk, and whisk until completely smooth.
* Lightly brush pan with oil.
* Once the oil is hot, pour in some of the batter and swirl to thinly coat the pan. A 5- cm ice-cream scoop provides the perfect measure.
* Once the edges of the pancake start to shrink inwards and the base is lightly golden, flip the pancake over.
* Cook until golden brown.
* Transfer to a baking sheet and repeat the entire process (including brushing the pan with a little oil) until you have used up all the batter.
* Cover the stack of pancakes with foil to keep them warm while you prepare the syrup.
* Place the sugar, water, honey, rose water, and saffron strands in a small saucepan over a high heat.
* Stir until the sugar has dissolved and then allow to come to the boil.
* Leave to simmer for about 6–8 minutes, stirring occasionally until slightly thickened.
* Turn off the heat, stir in the cardamom, and allow the syrup to cool a little.
* In the meantime, grind the pistachios.
* When the syrup is cool enough to handle, start assembling the baklava.
* Unwrap the pancakes from the foil and place the stack on a plate.
* Line a baking sheet with foil and place a pancake in the middle.
* Drizzle some syrup over and place a second pancake on top.
* Generously scatter with ground pistachios and lots more syrup.
* Repeat the process: add pancake/syrup/pancake/pistachios and syrup until you have used all the pancakes.

* Leave the top pancake plain without any syrup or pistachios.
* Wrap in the foil and bake in the preheated oven for 25 minutes.
* Allow to cool slightly on a rack.
* Slice using a sharp knife and serve warm alongside a scoop of your favourite ice cream. Drizzle with any remaining syrup and scatter on any extra pistachios.

Baklava Pancake Cake

AMERICAN STYLE PANCAKES WITH AN INDIAN TWIST

(Serves 4)

There are so many types of flatbreads prepared across India. Most of them are savoury, but some of them are sweet. Mum used to make Meetha Parantha for us when we were younger, and I suppose they are the Gujarati version of the more popular malpua, a Bengali pancake that is now served across India. Whereas malpua are made using rice flour, these slightly-easier-to-make parantha use wheat flour and are a thicker pancake. They are similar to what the West knows as American pancakes.

Ingredients

60 g jaggery
150 ml water
½ tsp ghee
80 g chapatti flour or plain flour
extra oil or ghee for frying
300g strawberries
4 tbsp demerara sugar
4 tsp rose water
½ tsp ground cardamom
cream to serve

* Prepare the batter by placing the jaggery and 120 ml of the water in a saucepan over a medium heat.
* Stir constantly until the jaggery has melted and the ingredients are well combined. Set aside to cool for 5 minutes.
* Stir in the ghee.
* Gradually add the flour, mixing well until the batter is pancake-like. At this stage, if the batter seems too thick, slowly add the remaining water until it reaches the pancake consistency.
* Place a flat, non-stick pan over a medium heat, and when hot, ladle one quarter of the batter into the middle of the pan.
* Use the back of the ladle to lightly spread the mixture around into approximately a 13-cm pancake.
* Drizzle some oil or ghee around the edges and over the surface of the pancake.
* When the edges of the pancake start to brown, flip the pancake over.
* Drizzle some more oil or ghee as before.
* Cook until golden on both sides.
* Transfer to a plate lined with paper towel while you fry the remaining pancakes.
* Repeat the above process with the remaining batter.
* Place each pancake on a plate.
* Hull and halve the strawberries, then arrange them on top of the pancakes—as many as you like on each.
* Sprinkle a tbsp of demerara sugar over each pancake and drizzle on the rose water.
* Place each plate under a hot grill, melting the sugar and cooking the strawberries slightly while heating everything through, about 3 minutes for each plate.
* Carefully remove from the grill (the plates will be hot), sprinkle on some cardamom, drizzle on some cream, and serve immediately.

American Style Pancakes With An Indian Twist

STEAMED SPONGE CAKE

(Serves 8)

As a child, I was always baffled that people would serve up a plate of dhokra and refer to them as a "spicy cake." The dhokra did, however, taste delicious. Since I started baking, it became wondrous to see how the egg-free batter magically rises in a steamer to produce a marvellously aerated, cake like sponge. Being loyal to my sweet tooth though, I had to try to replicate this effect with a non-savoury recipe and here it is. This steamed sponge cake is great served with a cup of tea.

Ingredients
150 g self raising flour
½ tsp baking powder
½ tsp salt
113 ml vegetable oil
125 g caster sugar
2 tsp vanilla extract
260 ml hot water
1 tsp bicarbonate of soda
1 tsp fruit salt
1 tbsp cocoa powder

Method
* Get the steamer ready with water and place on a medium heat.
* Grease and line a 20cm cake tin and place in the lowest section of the steamer so it can heat up while you prepare the cake batter.
* Sift the flour, baking powder, and salt into a mixing bowl.
* In a separate bowl, combine the oil, sugar, and vanilla extract. Mix well before adding the hot water and whisking thoroughly so that the sugar dissolves and the mixture is well combined.
* Pour the wet ingredients into the dry and whisk to combine.
* Add the bicarbonate of soda and fruit salt. Whisk well but quickly into the mixture.
* Pour the cake batter directly into the cake tin inside the steamer.
* Sprinkle with the cocoa powder.
* Close the steamer and allow to cook for 25–30 minutes until the surface is golden.
* Cool on a wire rack. Remove from tin and serve warm.

Steamed Sponge Cake

APRICOT AND SAFFRON SCONES

(Makes 12)

The flavour of these scones is very Mediterranean and inspired by the most northern, Persian-influenced regions of India. Centuries ago, farmers who travelled via the Middle East brought lots of new recipes and foods with them to India. These ingredients have since become part of the Indian diet, and are still reflected today in some aspects of Indian cuisine. Kashmiri saffron is one of the rarest and most sought after varieties in the world.

Ingredients

For the scones
225 g self raising flour
a pinch of salt
40 g caster sugar
75 g butter
50 g soft dried apricots (chopped into small chunks)
¼ tsp saffron
5 tbsp yoghurt

For the cream filling
250 ml double cream
2 tbsp honey
3 tbsp caster sugar
2 tbsp pistachios (chopped roughly)

Method

* Sift the flour and salt into a mixing bowl and add the sugar. Combine with a whisk.
* Cube the butter, and then rub it into the flour until the mixture resembles coarse breadcrumbs.
* Add the apricots and saffron.
* Beat the yoghurt until smooth, and then add it to the flour mixture and combine it using a palette knife.
* Knead the dough quickly to make sure it is well combined and that it is soft but not sticky. (If the dough feels too dry, add a little more yoghurt; and if it feels too sticky, add a little flour.)
* Allow to rest at room temperature for 15 minutes while you heat the oven to gas mark 7/220°C/425°F.
* Gently roll out the dough on a floured surface to about 2-cm thick.
* Use a 6-cm cookie cutter to press out the scones. Do not twist the cutter, just tap it through the dough once and lift straight out, this will help the scones to rise straight upwards.
* Arrange the scones on a lined baking sheet. Bake for 10 minutes until well risen and lightly golden.
* Transfer to a wire rack to cool.
* Prepare the cream filling by whipping the cream until soft peaks form. Fold in the honey, sugar, and pistachios.
* When the scones have cooled completely, slice them in half horizontally.
* Divide the cream filling equally between the 12 bottom halves of the scones.
* Place the tops on the scones and sprinkle with a little icing sugar if desired.
* Serve immediately or refrigerate until required.

Apricot and Saffron Scones

COCONUT AND RASPBERRY NANKHATAI

(Makes approximately 20)

My grandmother used to love making biscuits and was renowned throughout her community for the baked goodies she would bring along to social gatherings. Back in East Africa where she grew up, ovens were not available at the time so she would use a huge coal furnace with metal baking sheets. She would direct the process while the children (my aunts) would roll and cut the pastry. Her efforts resulted in hundreds of perfectly even biscuits, enough to feed all the families in the vicinity. My grandmother would swap some of these biscuits for wares made by the local women. As a result, everybody would have a fair share of a tremendous banquet of snacks come festival time. These little shortbread-style biscuits make great gifts for friends and family on special occasions.

Ingredients

115 g unsalted butter
70 g icing sugar
1/4 tsp ground cardamom
2 tbsp desiccated coconut
160 g plain flour
¼ tsp baking powder
¼ tsp salt
raspberries and white chocolate for decoration

Method

* Preheat oven to gas mark 2/150°C/300°F.
* Beat the butter in a large mixing bowl and then gradually add the icing sugar, fully incorporating it into the butter.
* Add the ground cardamom and desiccated coconut, and beat well to combine.
* In a separate bowl, sift together the flour, baking powder, and salt.
* Gradually beat the flour mixture into the butter mixture.
* When you have smooth, pliable dough, wrap it in plastic and leave to rest in the fridge for around 15 minutes.
* In the meantime prepare the baking sheet by lightly greasing it or lining it with parchment paper.
* Lightly knead the dough again and then divide into 16 equal pieces. (Make larger ones if desired; you'll just have fewer biscuits.)
* Roll each piece of dough into a smooth, round ball. It should not have any cracks on the surface.
* Place each dough ball onto the baking sheet, leaving about 3cm between each one as they will spread during baking.
* At this stage, press half a raspberry into the middle of each ball, if you like. Otherwise just use a finger to create a dimple there instead.
* Bake for 20–25 minutes. These biscuits should be white. Remove them from the oven before they become golden or they'll be extremely hard.
* Cool the biscuits on the baking sheet placed on a cooling rack.
* Drizzle with melted white chocolate or even dip the biscuits in the chocolate. Allow to set at room temperature.

Coconut and Raspberry Nankhatai

PISTACHIO AND COCONUT BISCUITS

(Makes 25–30)

These rustic biscuits are deliciously flavourful and incredibly easy to make. Almost like amoretti, the biscuits are quite brittle due to the quantity of nuts but taste great, especially if dipped in dark chocolate before serving.

Ingredients

100 g self raising flour
80 g caster sugar
100 g butter (cubed and at room temperature)
75 g ground pistachios
25 g desiccated coconut
¼ tsp ground cardamom

Method

* Sift the flour and sugar into a mixing bowl, and cut in the butter until well combined.
* Knead in the pistachios, coconut, and cardamom until you have a thoroughly mixed, dry dough.
* Roll into a log approximately 30-cm long and 3-cm in diameter.
* Wrap tightly in plastic wrap and allow to firm up in the fridge for at least one hour.
* Preheat oven to gas mark 4/180°C/350°F.
* Cut the log into 1-cm thick slices and place them onto a lined baking sheet making sure you leave 3cm between the biscuits for them to spread.
* Bake for 15 minutes until the edges are just firm but the middles are still quite soft (they will harden as they cool).
* Cool on a wire rack.

Pistachio and Coconut Biscuits

DATE AND COCONUT PALMIERS (ELEPHANT EARS)

(Makes 30)

Due to its long life, dried fruit is very popular in the northern regions of India where in the past; kings would send armies out across the hot, dry lands to battle for more ground. On these missions, the armies would carry rations of dried fruit and nuts to provide them with energy along the way. On another note, elephants are one of the most popular animals in India so this incredibly simple dried-fruit recipe with its resemblance to elephant ears is a perfectly fitting tea time treat. They are great for children.

Ingredients
200 g dates
4 tbsp double cream
50 g desiccated coconut
500 g puff pastry
1 tbsp icing sugar
1 tsp ground cinnamon

Method
* Add the dates and 2 tbsp of the double cream to a heavy-based saucepan. Place over a gentle heat and cover.
* Allow the dates to stew and soften, stirring occasionally until moist. This can take around 15 minutes, but don't be tempted to turn up the heat as this will burn the dates.
* Place the dates into a food processor and add the remaining cream and desiccated coconut.
* Pulse together until the mixture is finely crumbled. (Do not let it turn to paste.)
* On a floured surface, roll out the pastry to a rectangle approximately 30 cm x 40 cm (around 3 mm thick).
* Sprinkle the date mixture over the pastry.
* Position the pastry so that you have the two short sides facing you and the long sides on your left and right.
* Carefully and tightly roll the left side toward the middle of the pastry.
* Carefully and tightly roll the right side toward the middle of the pastry so that both sides meet in the centre.
* Brush a little milk down the line in the middle to stick both sides of the pastry together.
* Carefully wrap the rolled pastry tightly in plastic wrap and refrigerate for at least 1 hour.
* Preheat oven to gas mark 6/200°C/400°F, and line a baking sheet with greaseproof paper.
* Remove the roll from the fridge, unwrap the plastic, and carefully slice roll into 1 cm thick pieces (short end to short end).
* Lay the pieces on the baking sheet and bake for about 15 minutes until puffed and golden.
* Place on a wire rack to cool.
* Combine the icing sugar and cinnamon and generously sprinkle over the palmiers while they are still hot.
* Serve at room temperature.

Date and Coconut Palmiers

SWEET TREATS

Whenever you walk into an Indian sweet store, you are confronted with a variety of little bite-sized delicacies. They are lovely to look at, and their flavours are so rich and intense that a little goes a long way. This chapter is dedicated to these sweet nibbles—some traditionally Indian and some with an updated twist.

DRIED FRUIT GHOOGRA

(Makes 12)

Another recipe adapted from my grandmother, ghoogra, are little parcels of pastry that are stuffed with a roasted semolina-and-pistachio filling, and then deep fried to create a short flaky crust. Traditionally the edges are pleated around so they look like bells—hence the name "ghoogra," which is Gujarati for "tiny little jingle bells." I developed this baked version filled with dried fruits as a healthier option. The dried fruit needs no added sweetener, and obviously baking is far better for us than frying. The baked pastry is a little drier than the fried version but perfectly complements the softened fruit inside. If this is a bit too healthy, add some dark chocolate chips to the filling or sprinkle the pastries with cinnamon sugar and cocoa.

Ingredients

50 g plain flour
2½ tsp vegetable oil
30 ml cold water
40 g dates
25 g soft dried apricots
1 tbsp ground pistachios
2 tbsp desiccated coconut

Method

* Sift the flour into a small mixing bowl and mix in the oil.
* Knead into a smooth, soft but slightly dry dough with the water. Add a little more or less if necessary.
* Wrap in plastic wrap and set aside to rest while you prepare the filling.
* Combine the dates and apricots in a heavy-based saucepan with about 2 tbsp of water.
* Place over a low heat, cover, and allow to stew for about 10 minutes.
* Stir the fruit occasionally so it doesn't burn. Don't cook the fruit just soften it slightly.
* Place the softened fruit in a food processor and pulse into small chunks.
* Fold in the ground pistachios and desiccated coconut, and leave the mixture to cool completely.
* Preheat oven to gas mark 4/180°C/350°F.
* Roll the dough out until it is about 2-mm thick, and use a 7-cm cookie cutter (I used a half cup measuring cup) to cut out circles. Keep rolling and cutting until you have used all the dough to create 10–12 circles.
* Place about 2 tsp of the filling in the middle of each circle.
* Fold the circles into semicircles, and seal the pastries by pinching and fluting the edges. If this proves too fiddly, press them down with a fork instead.
* Place the pastries on a lined baking sheet and bake for 20 minutes until lightly golden.
* Serve warm or at room temperature.

Dried Fruit Ghoogra

CHOCOLATE MALAI KHAJA

(Makes 4–6)

Malai khaja are sweet delicacies that were introduced to India by the Mughals. While flatbreads have long been made in India, many Indian recipes that include pastry, such as sweet and more complex bread recipes, appear to have travelled to the sub-continent from the Middle East where this type of baking is far more common. These little parcels of sweetened milk curd come wrapped in layers of thin, flaky pastry that, like baklava, are then soaked in a sugar syrup. Here's the simple way of creating them using ready-made puff pastry.

Ingredients
1 L whole milk
2 tbsp lemon juice
4 tbsp cocoa
2 tbsp icing sugar
4 tbsp roughly chopped pistachios
150 g puff pastry
2 tbsp honey
50 ml water
pinch of ground cardamom

Method
* Start by using the milk and lemon juice to make the paneer or malai part of the recipe as directed on page 6.
* Place the drained paneer in a food processor along with the cocoa and icing sugar.
* Blend until smooth and then fold in the pistachios.
* Roll the pastry into a 20 cm x 10 cm rectangle and cut into 8 equal squares.
* Divide the paneer mixture between the squares, placing it in the middle of each one.
* Fold the corners of each square towards the centre so that they cover the chocolate malai, and place each parcel on a lined baking sheet.
* Refrigerate for 30 minutes. In the meantime, preheat oven to gas mark 6/200°C/400°F.
* Bake the malai khaja for 20 minutes until puffed and golden.
* While the khaja are baking, prepare the syrup. Place the honey and water in a saucepan and warm through until the honey almost dissolves to produce a sweetened but runny syrup.
* Turn off the heat and stir in the cardamom.
* When the khaja are baked, transfer them to a wire rack to cool and generously drizzle with the syrup.
* Serve just slightly warm or at room temperature.

Chocolate Malai Khaja

BALUSHAHI

(Makes 16)

I find this recipe is adored by the fathers of families, mine included. The firm, bread-like texture of these dumplings makes them quite similar to donuts so when soaked in the syrup it creates a glaze on top unlike their softer cousin, gulab jamun which absorbs the syrup to become saturated.

Ingredients

240 g plain flour
2 tbsp cocoa
¼ tsp salt
120 g unsalted butter
¼ tsp bicarbonate of soda
8 tbsp yoghurt
200 g caster sugar
250 ml water
10 g pistachios, chopped

Method

* Sift the flour, cocoa, and salt into a large mixing bowl and combine using a whisk.
* Rub the butter into the flour until the mixture resembles breadcrumbs.
* In a separate bowl add the bicarbonate of soda to 5 tbsp of the yogurt. Beat until smooth, and then add to the flour mixture.
* Knead into a smooth, soft dough adding the remaining yoghurt if required. The dough will start off quite sticky but will become stiffer as you knead it. Knead for about 5–8 minutes.
* Place the dough back into the mixing bowl, cover with cling film, and leave to rest for 1 hour.
* Heat about 8 cm of oil over a fairly low setting. Do not fry the dough too quickly or it won't cook from inside.
* Divide the dough into 16 equal portions, and roll into smooth balls, taking care not to overwork the dough.
* Press thumb into the centre of each ball to indent.
* Slowly and carefully fry the balls of dough until they turn a deep golden brown.
* Leave aside to cool slightly.
* While the balushahi are cooling, prepare the sugar syrup. Heat the sugar and water together in a wide, heavy-based saucepan.
* Cook for about 15 minutes or until slightly sticky.
* Carefully transfer the balushahi into the hot sugar syrup.
* Allow to soak for about 5 minutes on each side before using a slotted spoon to carefully transfer them to a serving dish.
* Sprinkle the pistachios on top and serve slightly warm or at room temperature.

Balushahi

CHOCOLATE AND HAZELNUT LADOO

(Makes 18)

Another popular sweet in India is the ladoo. These come in many flavours, colours, and sizes and can be made from a variety of ingredients including gram flour, wheat flour, and semolina. One thing they all have in common is that they are always round. Barfi differs in that it comes in all shapes and forms, but ladoos are always spheres of sweet goodness. Ladoos are often used to celebrate religious occasions. For some reason children seem to prefer the shapes and colours of barfi, so I created this chocolate ladoo to entice the younger generation.

Ingredients

200 g sweetened condensed milk
1 tbsp cocoa
2 tbsp milk
100 g milk powder
100 g milk chocolate
1 tbsp chocolate hazelnut spread
60 g hazelnuts, roasted and coarsely chopped

Method

* Combine the condensed milk, cocoa, and milk in a wok, and heat gently until smooth and well combined.
* Sift in the milk powder and stir until the mixture forms a smooth, soft dough that comes away easily from the sides of the pan.
* Leave the mixture aside until it is cool enough to handle but still warm and pliable.
* Taking one tbsp of the dough at a time roll into a smooth ball and place onto a wire rack to cool completely. Make about 18 balls.
* When the ladoos are completely cold, melt the chocolate gently in a microwave or in a bowl set above a larger bowl of simmering water.
* Stir the hazelnut spread into the chocolate and make sure that the mixture is not too hot but warm enough so that it is runny.
* Working on two or three ladoos at a time, dip them into the melted chocolate to coat lightly, and then transfer to the bowl of roasted hazelnuts.
* Shake the bowl to coat the ladoos in hazelnuts, and then transfer them to a lined baking sheet.
* When all the ladoos are complete, chill in the refrigerator for 30 minutes to set the chocolate. Serve at room temperature.

Chocolate and Hazelnut Ladoo

COCONUT AND PINEAPPLE SANDESH TRUFFLES

(Makes 18)

Originally from the Bengal region of India, sandesh is a sweet made from fresh paneer that has been lightly spiced and rolled into balls. Its creamy softness makes the consistency very truffle-like so they are incredibly moreish. The tropical flavour of pineapple is fairly new to India as they have only recently begun to be cultivated there. The sweet-and-sour aroma fits in perfectly with Indian tastes, and it has become a well-loved delicacy.

Ingredients

1 L whole milk
2 tbsp lemon juice
50 g caster sugar
4 tbsp coconut milk
30 g dried pineapple (finely chopped)
¼ tsp ground cardamom
100 g white chocolate
10 g desiccated coconut
10 g popping candy

Method

* Using the milk and lemon juice, make paneer as directed on page 6.
* Turn the paneer out into a mixing bowl, and combine with the sugar.
* Mix to form a grainy paste.
* Transfer to a non-stick frying pan and add the coconut milk.
* Cook over a low heat, stirring continuously until the milk has evaporated and the paneer forms a smooth, soft dough that comes easily away from the pan.
* Turn off the heat, and fold in the finely chopped pineapple and the cardamom powder.
* Taking a tbsp of the dough at a time, roll into smooth balls, and allow to cool completely in the fridge.
* Gently melt the white chocolate, taking care to ensure that it does not get too hot otherwise it will burn and become grainy.
* Dip each sandesh in white chocolate to cover and leave on greaseproof paper to set.
* Sprinkle on the popping candy and refrigerate.
* Serve chilled.

Coconut and Pineapple Sandesh Truffles

CHIKKI

(Serves 6)

Chikki is very much like a peanut brittle but is made using a jaggery caramel. The darker the caramel, the harder the finished product will be. Mum always taught me to make the caramel quite light to produce a soft, chewy chikki, but if you prefer more of a crunch, just let the melted jaggery darken slightly before adding the nuts. This is one of our favourite snacks at home, something that everybody likes, which is arguably healthy and incredibly tasty.

Ingredients

50 g shelled pistachios
50 g cashews
50 g peanuts
50 g almonds
175 g jaggery
1 tbsp ghee
50 g chocolate (milk or dark)

Method

* Start by dry roasting the nuts. Put them all into a large frying pan and place over a fairly high heat.
* Roast, tossing constantly until fragrant, lightly coloured, and crunchy.
* Transfer to a plate and allow to cool.
* Line a baking sheet with greaseproof paper and keep close to hand.
* Add the ghee and jaggery to the frying pan used to roast the nuts and allow them to melt over a medium heat, stirring occasionally.
* When the jaggery has melted and is just starting to bubble slightly, add the nuts and stir well to combine.
* Ensure that all the nuts have been coated in the caramel and then carefully transfer the mixture to the lined baking sheet.
* Use a rolling pin to spread the mixture into a sheet about 1-cm thick. (Take care as the chikki will be extremely hot. Work quickly or it will begin to set.)
* When the chikki has cooled slightly use a sharp knife to score it into 3 x 3 cm squares.
* Gently melt the chocolate.
* When the chikki is cool cut the previously scored squares and dip the back of the pieces into the chocolate.
* After dipping return each square to the lined baking sheet and allow the chocolate to set.
* Serve at room temperature.

Chikki

SHAHI BARFI

(Makes 25 pieces)

Shahi, meaning "royal" is often applied to dishes from the northern Mughal-influenced areas of India like Rajasthan. This region has a heritage of royal palaces and monarchies. Cuisine from this region normally contains lots of different dried fruit and nuts, floral essences, and silver "warq" (leaf). This quick and easy shahi barfi recipe adds these regal ingredients to our favourite sweet treat, barfi. Feel free to dress them with silver or gold leaf for that extra royal experience.

Ingredients

398 g tin sweetened condensed milk
1 tbsp rose water
20 g plain shelled pistachios, roughly chopped
20 g almonds, roughly chopped
10 g cashews, roughly chopped
2 tbsp raisins
250 g milk powder
1 tsp ground cardamom

Method

* Line a square 15-cm baking dish with greaseproof paper.
* Place the condensed milk and rose water in a non-stick pan over a low heat and gently warm.
* Add the nuts and raisins and let the mixture warm through.
* Sift in the milk powder.
* Cook the mixture until the liquid has absorbed and you are left with a smooth, moist dough.
* Turn off the heat and mix in the cardamom.
* Turn the dough out into the prepared baking dish and level.
* Leave aside or refrigerate until cold and set.
* Cut into square or diamond shapes and serve at room temperature.

Shahi Barfi

COCONUT AND ROSE BARFI

(Makes 25 pieces)

Barfi is one of the most popular traditional Indian sweets. There are so many different ways of making barfi, and it can be flavoured with almost anything. One of my personal favourites is rose as it reminds me of the rose-flavoured milk Mum used to give me during the summer holidays when I was young. Coconut complements the floral hints of rose by introducing a more full-bodied flavour.

Ingredients
398 g tin sweetened condensed milk
2 tbsp rose water
30 g desiccated coconut
200 g milk powder
a few drops of pink food colouring (optional)

Method
* Line a square 15-cm baking dish with greaseproof paper.
* Place the condensed milk and rose water in a non-stick pan over a low heat and gently warm until slightly thickened, usually around 5 minutes.
* Stir in the food colouring if using. (Remember the shade will lighten slightly when the other ingredients are added so colour the mixture accordingly.)
* Stir in the desiccated coconut until evenly spread throughout the milk.
* Sift in the milk powder and cook the mixture until the liquid has absorbed. The dough should be smooth and moist but not too wet.
* Turn the dough out into the prepared baking dish and level.
* Leave aside or refrigerate until cold and set.
* Cut into square or diamond shapes and serve at room temperature.

Coconut and Rose Barfi

CHOCOLATE JALEBI

(Makes approximately 10)

The elusive jalebi- It can be found in almost every Indian sweet shop but how do they make it? Often referred to as India's national sweet dish and known for its vibrant orange colour, this tasty delight is best served fresh and hot. This recipe comes from wondering and gazing in awe at the "jalebi wallahs" (people who make jalebi) while they expertly spiral never-ending noodles of batter into vast vats of hot oil as I eagerly await my box of freshly made sweet orange amazingness.

Ingredients

120 g plain flour
80 g fine semolina
a pinch of baking powder
½ tsp yoghurt
750 ml warm water
orange food colouring (optional)
325 g caster sugar
a few saffron strands
¼ tsp ground cardamom
vegetable oil (for deep frying)
200 g good quality dark chocolate, chopped

Method

* Sift the flour, semolina and baking powder into a large mixing bowl.
* Mix the yoghurt in until well combined.
* Take 375 ml of the warm water and add it to the flour mixture a little at a time until there's a smooth runny batter that doesn't ribbon as it pours.
* Cover the bowl with cling film and leave in a warm place for a minimum of 2 hours or overnight. (The mixture should have risen considerably.)
* Heat the sugar and remaining water in a wide, heavy-bottomed saucepan with the saffron.
* Keep over a medium heat for about 15 minutes until slightly sticky and visibly thickened.
* Turn off the heat and stir in the cardamom and 1 or 2 drops of orange food colouring.
* Fill about 6cm of oil in a deep frying pan and place over a high heat.
* Whisk 1 or 2 drops of orange food colouring into the jalebi batter, and then pour some of the batter into a piping bag.
* Cut a small hole about 2–3 mm wide at the end of the piping bag and pipe the batter straight into the frying pan. The oil should be really hot so be careful, and be quick so they don't stick. Do 1 or 2 at a time.
* Pipe the batter in concentric circles ending in a "full stop" at the centre.
* Fry for a few seconds on each side until they are golden and firm, and then remove onto a paper towel to drain the oil.
* When all the jalebis have been fried, warm the sugar syrup again and place the jalebis into it.
* Leave to soak for a few minutes on each side before removing and transferring to a wire rack to drain slightly.
* Gently melt the chocolate in a microwave or in a bowl set above a larger bowl containing simmering water.
* Serve hot jalebi and melted chocolate together, fondue style.

Chocolate Jalebi

SWEET KACHORI

(Makes about 15)

These are normally a savoury snack stuffed with peas or lentils but they go down so well at all of my family dinners that I thought it might be fun to create a sweet version. The pastry is very similar to a normal shortcrust. It's crispy and crumbly at the same time, although dry. That is the reason that the sweetened paneer and melted chocolate filling complement it so well. I am pleased to say that these kachori now disappear just as quickly as the savoury ones. Success!

Ingredients

1 L whole milk
1 tbsp lemon juice
30 g caster sugar (or to taste)
2 tbsp chocolate chips
2 tbsp chopped pistachios
½ tsp ground cardamom
200 g plain flour
2 tbsp vegetable oil
150 ml warm water
oil for frying

Method

* Start by making the paneer for the filling by using the milk and lemon juice and following the recipe on page 6.
* While the paneer drains, make the dough. Sift the flour into a mixing bowl.
* Add the oil and rub in to the flour.
* Add half of the water to the flour and knead into a smooth, soft dough that isn't sticky but isn't dry either. Use the remaining water as required.
* Cover and leave aside to rest for at least 15 minutes or until the filling is ready.
* Place the dried paneer into a food processor and pulse 3 or 4 times just to make it slightly smooth and sticky enough so that it holds together when pressed.
* Add the sugar to taste.
* Fold the chocolate chips, nuts, and cardamom into the paneer.
* Taking about 1/2 tsp of the mixture at a time, roll into 15 balls.
* Divide the dough into 15 sections and taking one at a time roll into 8-cm circles. (Do not use extra flour on the rolling surface. Dough should be just dry enough not to stick.)
* Place a ball of the filling in the middle of the pastry circle and bring up the sides of the pastry to encase the filling.
* Pinch the dough at the top to remove any excess and leave covered with a tea towel while you prepare the rest of the kachori.
* Place about 7cm of oil in a pan over a moderate heat. To check if the oil is ready, put a piece of dough into the pan; it should sink to the bottom, slowly rise after about 2 seconds, and then gradually brown.
* Fry the kachori until they are lightly golden and the pastry appears slightly bobbly.
* Sprinkle on a little icing sugar if desired and serve warm.

Sweet Kachori

APPLE CHUTNEY SAMOSAS

(Makes 8, Serves 4)

The boys in my family love apple pie just as much as they love samosas so this recipe was a no-brainer. Spiced a little more like apple chutney (especially for Dad) and wrapped in samosa pastry, these golden triangles have a somewhat homely, comforting, and reviving air about them. Just the thought of them lifts my spirits as they remind me of my family. If you've never made samosas before, use circles of paper to practice the pastry- folding technique described below.

Ingredients

For the Filling
1 Granny Smith apple
1 Pink Lady apple
1 tbsp butter
1 tbsp lemon juice
25 g dark muscovado sugar
25 g caster sugar
¼ tsp ground cloves
¾ tsp ground ginger
1 tsp ground cinnamon
3 tbsp flaked almonds
2 tbsp chocolate chips

For the Pastry
80 g plain flour
¼ tsp salt
1 tsp lemon juice
4–5 tbsp ice-cold water
vegetable oil

For the Pastry "Glue"
1 tbsp plain flour
2–3 tbsp cold water

For the Cinnamon Sugar
4 tbsp icing sugar
2 tsp ground cinnamon

Method
* Peel the apples and chop into 1-cm cubes.
* Add the lemon juice to the apples and toss to lightly coat all of the pieces.
* Warm the butter in a heavy-bottomed saucepan over a medium heat.
* When the butter has melted add the apples, sugars, clove, ginger, and cinnamon.
* Allow to simmer for 5 minutes, stirring occasionally.
* Turn up the heat and allow the juices that have formed in the pan to come to the boil.
* Simmer over a high temperature for a further 2–3 minutes until the apples are soft but still have a bit of bite to them.
* Turn off the heat, cover the pan, and allow to cool completely. Leave it for 3–4 hours.

Pastry
* Sift the flour and salt into a small mixing bowl.
* Add the lemon juice and bind using the cold water as needed. The dough should be smooth, soft and white without having to work it too much.
* Wrap the dough in plastic wrap and allow to rest in the fridge for 10 minutes.
* Place a flat frying pan over a medium heat.
* Divide the dough into 4 sections and roll each into a 10-cm round.
* Place the rounds in a damp tea towel to prevent them from drying out.
* Spread the surface of one of the rounds with about ½ tsp vegetable oil and place a second round on top.
* Roll the two rounds together to form one large 20-cm flatbread.
* Place a flatbread on the hot frying pan and roast until little bubbles start to appear on the surface and the colour just changes. Do not let the flatbread brown.
* Return roasted flatbread to the damp tea towel and very carefully, using the tip of a knife, pull the two flatbreads apart.
* Stack with the oiled sides facing away from each other.
* Repeat with the other two small rounds to end up with 4 large rounds.
* Keep the pastry stored in the damp tea towel until you are ready to fry the samosas.

Assembly

* Place about 7 cm of oil to heat up to a high temperature in a medium-sized frying pan.
* Strain the apple mixture to get rid of the excess liquid and fold the almonds and chocolate chips into the apple mixture.
* In a small bowl, mix together the flour and water for the "glue" to form a sticky, runny paste.
* To assemble the samosas, take 1 circle of the pastry and cut in half.
* Place a strip of the pastry roasted side down, and make a point in the middle.
* Bring the bottom right corner of the pastry up to the middle of the top edge so that it makes a straight line down the centre of the pastry.
* Use a brush to spread some "glue" along the left edge of the pastry.
* Bring the bottom left corner up and over so that it forms a sharp point at the middle of the bottom edge.
* Press the glued edge down to seal it into position, forming a pastry cone.
* Lift the cone and turn it around. Open up the top and fill with about a tbsp of the apple mixture.
* Apply some "glue" to the top flaps and bring them over to seal in the apples.
* Repeat with the rest of the pastry so you are left with 8 samosas.
* Deep fry in the preheated oil until golden brown on both sides, drain on kitchen paper.
* Combine the sugar and cinnamon for the cinnamon sugar, and sprinkle generously over the samosas while they are still hot.
* Enjoy warm.

Apple Chutney Samosas

FRUIT PAKORAS

(Serves 6)

Weekends at home always meant making a batch of my grandmother's savoury fritters—her favourite food in the world. From onion bhaji to vegetable pakoras, spiced potato fritters, and even aubergines—nearly everything got the batter treatment; and I'd be lying if I said I didn't enjoy them all. As a family we loved those Saturday evenings enjoying the vegetable dishes. The logical progression was fruit pakoras for dessert. It's the same process, just a different batter. So, why not?

Ingredients

1 cooking apple
1 pear
1 banana
160 g plain flour
2 tsp corn flour
1 tsp lemon juice
250 ml ice-cold sparkling water
2 tsp ground cinnamon
2 tbsp icing sugar
sunflower oil for deep frying

Method

* Heat up 6-cm of sunflower oil in a wok over a medium/high temperature.
* While the oil heats, peel the fruit, and chop into 1-cm cubes. Leave aside.
* Sift the flour and corn flour into a large mixing bowl.
* Pour in the lemon juice and cold water and mix to create a smooth batter.
* Stir in 1 tsp of the ground cinnamon.
* Fold in the fruit pieces.
* Carefully place several tsp of batter into the hot oil, leaving space between each one so they do not stick to each other. (The oil is hot enough if the batter sinks then immediately rises back up, with the oil bubbling away.)
* Fry until the fritters are golden all over, and then remove them from the oil, and leave to drain on some kitchen paper.
* When all the fritters have been fried, sprinkle on the icing sugar and the rest of the cinnamon, making sure that all the fritters get a good coating.
* Serve hot, with vanilla ice cream if desired.

Fruit Pakoras

AFTER-DINNER DESSERTS

(TRADITIONAL)

This is my favourite chapter. Indian desserts are sweet, fragrant, indulgent puddings that are served piping hot or perfectly chilled. Presented beautifully, they provide a stunning end to any meal and some of them, like seera and shrikhand are really easy to make.

BAKED GULAB JAMUN

(Makes 4)

One of the most well-loved Indian desserts, gulab jamun, is present at almost every celebration from weddings to festivals or even just after dinner for dessert. Who needs an excuse? These delectable spongy little spheres are one of my family's favourite desserts and I can remember my grandmother, Mum, aunts and even cousins experimenting with lots of different recipes to see whose came out best. This is my baked version which I think is just as good as Mum's but offers a little less guilt than the traditional deep-fried version.

Ingredients

60 g milk powder
2 tbsp plain flour
¼ tsp bicarbonate of soda
2 tbsp yoghurt
1 tbsp melted ghee (clarified butter)
200 g caster sugar
450 ml water
½ tsp saffron threads
½ tsp ground cardamom

Method

* Preheat oven to gas mark 4/180°C/350°F.
* Sift the milk powder, flour, and bicarbonate of soda into a mixing bowl, and make a well in the middle.
* Pour the yoghurt and ghee into the well and gradually combine with the dry ingredients. Then knead into a dough that is quite dry in consistency but still soft and smooth enough so that no cracks appear on the surface.
* Leave to rest for 20 minutes. In the meantime, grease 4 cavities of a muffin tray and prepare the sugar syrup.
* Place the sugar and water in a flat-based pan and put over a high heat.
* Stir until the sugar has dissolved and then bring to the boil.
* Turn the heat down a little, add the saffron strands, and simmer for 5–10 minutes until the syrup is lightly coloured and slightly sticky.
* Turn off the heat, stir in the cardamom, cover the syrup, and leave aside.
* Divide the dough into 4 equal portions.
* Lightly grease the palms of your hands, and roll the portions of dough into smooth balls without any cracks in them.
* Gently press each ball into a greased section of the muffin tray.
* Bake for 15–20 minutes until the gulab jamuns look lightly golden on the surface and a tooth pick inserted into the middle of each one comes out clean.
* When the gulab jamuns have baked, allow them to cool just until they are warm enough to handle, and then ease each one out of the muffin tin and place into the warm sugar syrup.
* Be sure to leave some space between each gulab jamun in the pan as they will expand as they soak up the syrup.
* Cover and leave to soak for 30 minutes and then carefully flip them over in the syrup so they can saturate from both sides.
* Cover and leave for at least another 30 minutes until completely soaked in the syrup.
* Serve warm with a scoop of vanilla or pistachio ice cream.

Baked Gulab Jamun

MOHANTHAAL

(Serves 6)

Mohanthaal is Mum's speciality. If my family knows that she is serving this for dessert, they will all be here well before the meal is even ready. This is a very traditional Gujarati pudding, served hot and sweet. I think we love it so much because Mum normally makes it at the festival of Diwali, which falls in October or November each year, just when the cold weather really starts setting in here, in England.

Ingredients

180 g coarse gram flour
135 g ghee or unsalted butter
180 g sugar
180 ml water
½ tsp saffron
120 ml evaporated milk
10 g ground pistachios
10 g ground almonds
½ tsp ground cardamom
200 ml double cream

Method

* Pour the gram flour into a bowl without sifting.
* Add 2 tsp each of the ghee and evaporated milk. Rub into the flour so that it resembles coarse breadcrumbs, and leave to soak for 10 minutes.
* Combine the sugar and water together in a small, heavy-based saucepan.
* Place over a medium heat and allow the sugar to dissolve before stirring in the saffron.
* Leave to thicken over a medium heat while you prepare the gram flour mixture. (Make sure to turn off the heat once the caramel becomes just slightly sticky, about 15 minutes.)
* Add the remaining ghee to a large wok or deep-frying pan and place over a medium heat
* Sift in the gram-flour mixture using a coarse sifter. (There will be some mixture that doesn't pass through the sifter. Crush this in the palms of your hands, and then add to the wok.)
* Cook the mixture, stirring often until it becomes fragrant and golden (about 5 minutes).
* Carefully add the remaining evaporated milk to the gram-flour mixture. It will bubble slightly and then the gram flour will begin to soak up the milk.
* Add the nuts and cardamom.
* Continue to cook the mixture, stirring often until all of the milk has been absorbed, and it really starts to roast and turns a deep amber gold colour.
* Very carefully pour the sugar syrup into the gram-flour mixture.
* Stir well to combine, and cook for about a minute more.
* Turn off the heat and allow to cool slightly before pouring into serving bowls.
* Serve hot drizzled generously with double cream.

Mohanthaal

SHAHI TUKRA (INDIAN BREAD PUDDING)

(Serves 4)

Shahi Tukra is the Indian version of the classic bread-and-butter pudding. Brought into India by the Moghuls, it is prominently known in the Rajasthan area of India and associated with royalty. The name itself means "royal piece," paying homage to its empirical origins. The dried fruits and nuts used in the dish are also a sign of the dish's royal roots, as these were often part of a soldier's rations when he went off to war to protect the monarchy.

Ingredients

800 ml whole milk
¼ tsp crushed saffron threads
50 ml double cream
75 g caster sugar
1 tbsp raisins
2 tbsp roughly chopped almonds
2 tbsp roughly chopped pistachios
1 tsp ground cardamom
4 slices thick-cut white bread
ghee for shallow frying
chocolate shavings to garnish

Method

* Pour the milk and saffron into a wide, heavy-bottomed saucepan placed over a medium heat.
* Cook the milk until it has reduced by half and thickened. This will take around 25 minutes.
* Stir the double cream, sugar, raisins, and chopped nuts into the milk and continue to heat, stirring occasionally over a low heat while preparing the bread.
* Trim the crusts from the slices of bread, and then cut each slice into 4 equal triangles.
* Heat up 1 tsp of ghee in a shallow frying pan over a high heat and fry the triangles of bread for a minute or two on each side until golden brown. Add more ghee to the pan when required.
* Arrange the slices of hot, fried bread in a large serving dish.
* Ensure the milk has reduced and thickened slightly. Switch off the heat and stir in the cardamom.
* Carefully pour the hot milk over the bread.
* Allow the bread to soak up the milk and become really moist and fragrant.
* Serve either piping hot or chilled, garnished with chocolate shavings and more chopped nuts if desired.

Shahi Tukra

GAJAR KA HALWA

(Serves 6)

This is another family favourite. This recipe has been carefully honed over the years by my aunts who absolutely love it. A hot carrot pudding might seem strange, but it really does work. The sweetness of the carrots is enhanced by caramelisation, and the added spices create the most intense, indulgent aroma. A lot of recipes make this dish with water, but that just doesn't do it for us at home, the use of milk creates a deliciously creamy texture, especially when paired with ice cream.

Ingredients
500 g carrots
2 tbsp ghee
170 g caster sugar
10 g almonds, halved
150 ml milk
¼ tsp crushed saffron threads
110 ml single cream
½ tsp coarsely ground almonds
½ tsp coarsely ground pistachios

Method
* Peel the carrots and finely grate them.
* Heat up the ghee in a wok over a medium high heat. Add the grated carrots and cook for about 15–20 minutes until tender.
* Add the sugar, and stir until it dissolves.
* Once the liquid from the sugar has evaporated, add the milk and saffron.
* Cook over a high heat until the milk has reduced by about three quarters (5–10 minutes).
* Stir in the cream, and continue to cook until the mixture thickens.
* Fold in the ground nuts.
* Reduce the heat to medium, and continue cooking until most of the liquid evaporates and there is a sweet, moist carrot mixture.
* Transfer to a serving dish and garnish with extra pistachio and almonds.
* Serve piping hot with a generous scoop of vanilla ice cream.

Gajar Ka Halwa

SWEET SAFFRON RICE

(Serves 4)

This dish is more for the grown-ups who prefer a spicier sweet treat at the end of a meal. Although a healthy recipe, it was another of Mum's standby meals for when we were being difficult about what to eat as children. She made a meal disguised as a dessert! For those who prefer a lighter dessert, the use of coconut milk and jaggery to flavour this delight makes it an ideal alternative to a heavy rice pudding.

Ingredients

200 g white basmati rice
1 tbsp ghee
4 cloves
200 ml coconut milk
350 ml water
100 g jaggery
½ tsp saffron
½ tsp cardamom
fresh or desiccated coconut to garnish

Method

* Start by washing the rice in warm water and then leave it to soak for 45 minutes.
* Warm up the ghee in a heavy-based pan over a medium heat.
* Add cloves and sauté to release the flavours.
* Drain the rice. Add it to the pan, and stir to coat in the ghee.
* Add the coconut milk, water, and saffron. Stir well. Turn up the heat and allow the rice to come to the boil.
* Reduce the heat to medium. Cover and leave to simmer for 5 minutes.
* Remove the lid. Stir the rice well, and allow to cook until the liquid has evaporated completely and the rice is tender.
* Stir in the sugar. Allow it to dissolve and any excess liquid to evaporate.
* Turn off the heat, and stir in the cardamom.
* Tightly press a quarter of the mixture into a bowl and then turn out the rice onto a serving plate. Garnish with coconut and/or some dried fruits. Repeat with the rest of the rice.
* Best served hot.

Sweet Saffron Rice

CHOCOLATE SEERA

(Serves 8)

Offered daily in Hindu and Sikh temples, seera is an all-time classic Indian dessert, which is incredibly easy to make and creates the perfect end to any meal. The most difficult thing about seera is getting everybody to agree on how they like it served. I love it hot with lots of sultanas, whereas my sister prefers it cold and leaves her share of sultanas aside for me to finish off. Whichever way you like it, seera is one of those comforting classics. It certainly takes me right back to my childhood whenever I taste it.

Ingredients

450 ml whole milk
90 g ghee (clarified butter)
125 g coarse semolina
160 g golden caster sugar
¼ tsp crushed saffron strands
1 tbsp chopped almonds
¼ tsp ground cardamom
20 g milk-chocolate chips (or your favourite chocolate, roughly chopped)

Method

* Grease and line a 15-cm (6") cake tin, or prepare some jelly moulds.
* Pour the milk into a saucepan, and put to warm up over a medium heat.
* In the meantime, warm up the ghee in a large wok over a medium heat.
* When the ghee is melted add the semolina and increase the heat.
* Roast the semolina until brown and nutty, stirring often.
* While the semolina is cooking, add the sugar and saffron to the warmed milk, and stir until the sugar has dissolved.
* When the semolina and milk are both ready, switch off the heat under the wok, and very carefully pour in the warm milk. Take extra care because it will bubble and splutter a bit.
* Turn the heat back up. Add the almonds, and stir constantly until the milk evaporates and the mixture starts to come away from the wok.
* Switch off the heat, and fold in the cardamom and chocolate chips.
* Transfer the seera to the prepared cake tin or moulds, and level the surface.
* After allowing the seera to cool for about 10 minutes, run a knife around the edge and turn out onto a plate. Serve with extra cream, nuts, and berries if desired.

Chocolate Seera

RASMALAI WITH STRAWBERRY COMPOTE

(Serves 6)

Rasmalai originates from Orissa in the Bengal region of India, but its irresistible deliciousness has allowed it to travel across the country and the world and it is now probably one of the most well-known and favoured Indian desserts of all time. The soft, melt-in-the-mouth, sponge-like ovals are the "malai," and the sweet, fragrant, delicately spiced milk is the "ras." This dessert takes time to make, but is well worth it; and you can even make it a day in advance if you are having a dinner party. Your guests will be stunned. The strawberry compote helps to liven up the colour and flavour slightly, but it is entirely optional.

Ingredients

For the Malai
1 L whole milk
2 tbsp lemon juice
1 L water
200 g caster sugar

For the Ras
500 ml whole milk
100 g caster sugar
¼ tsp crushed saffron threads
¼ vanilla pod
1 tbsp rose water
¼ tsp ground cardamom

For the Strawberry Compote
175 g strawberries
2 tbsp caster sugar
2 tbsp rose water
¼ tsp vanilla extract

Method

* The first part of this recipe is making the paneer, which will form the "malai." Use the whole milk and lemon juice, and follow the recipe on page 6.
* Place the drained paneer in a food processor with a chopping attachment, and blend until it comes together to form a smooth ball.
* Remove from the processor and knead gently until you have a completely smooth dough.
* Use a rounded dessert spoon to form 12 equal portions of the dough, and roll each into a smooth round ball with no cracks in it.
* Bring the 200 g sugar and water to the boil together inside a large pressure cooker
* Take each ball of the paneer and gently flatten it until it is approximately 1-cm thick.
* Place all of the paneer patties into the pressure cooker and allow them to cook over a medium heat until the whistle rises or for a maximum of 10 minutes.
* Allow the cooker to cool before you open it; and then use a serrated spoon to gently lift out each malai, and place it on a dish to cool slightly.
* While the malai are cooking and cooling, you can begin making the "ras." Bring the milk to the boil in a large non-stick saucepan over a high heat.
* When the milk has boiled, reduce the heat, add the sugar, saffron, rose water, and vanilla pod, and allow to simmer, stirring occasionally until the milk has reduced by one third (about 15 minutes).
* Turn off the heat and remove the vanilla pod from the milk.
* Stir in the cardamom, and allow to cool slightly.
* When both the ras and malai have cooled slightly but are still warm, gently squeeze out some of the excess sugar syrup from the malai by pressing them downwards, and then place each one into the ras.

- * Place in the refrigerator to chill completely.
- * To make the strawberry compote, hull and quarter the strawberries and place in a saucepan together with the sugar, rose water, and vanilla extract.
- * Warm over a low heat, stirring occasionally and allowing the strawberries to release their juice; and then let the mixture thicken a little (about 5 minutes).
- * Allow the compote to cool slightly before refrigerating.
- * To assemble the dessert, place a rasmalai on the centre of each dish, and top with a tsp of compote. Place another rasmalai on top, and garnish with a little extra compote and some chopped pistachios if desired. Serve chilled.

Rasmalai With Strawberry Compote

WHITE CHOCOLATE KHEER

(Serves 4-5)

This is Jay's all-time favourite dessert. The Indian version of rice pudding, traditionally served at religious ceremonies and celebrations, kheer is one of the most popular Indian desserts. It does take a lot of patience to stand and stir the milk over a low heat until the rice is cooked through, but the aroma that fills your kitchen is like no other and truly worth all the effort. Served cold after a hot and spicy meal, kheer really makes the perfect complement to a dinner party. The white chocolate adds extra richness, making it all the more special.

Ingredients

500 ml whole milk
50 g pudding/short grain rice
¼ tsp ghee
40 g caster sugar
¼ tsp crushed saffron threads
1 tbsp chopped pistachios
100 ml single cream
½ tsp ground cardamom
50 g white chocolate, roughly chopped

Method

* Place the milk to warm in a heavy-based saucepan over a medium heat.
* While the milk warms up, rinse the rice in cold water. Roughly dry the grains, and rub in the ghee, making sure all of the grains are lightly coated.
* When the milk is hot, add the rice, and allow to cook until completely tender, about 30-40 minutes over a medium heat.
* Stir in the sugar, saffron, and cream; and bring to the boil over a low/medium heat.
* Switch off the heat and allow to cool while stirring every few minutes so that a skin doesn't form on top.
* When the kheer has cooled slightly but is still warm, stir in the white chocolate and cardamom. The white chocolate should melt through and combine with the kheer.
* When the kheer has cooled completely, cover it, and place in the fridge to chill for at least 2 hours.
* Serve chilled with some scattered pistachios or grated chocolate if desired.

White Chocolate Kheer

PEACH SHRIKHAND

(Serves approximately 4)

This sweet, rich, and creamy summer classic is similar to something between an ice cream and an Eton mess. It's delicious with most kinds of soft fruits from berries to mangoes, but in this recipe I'm serving it with juicy peaches for that classic summer flavour of peaches and cream. Try sprinkling some crumbled ginger biscuits on top for extra texture.

Ingredients

500 g thick-set yoghurt
350 g icing sugar
2 tbsp finely chopped roasted pistachios
4 tinned peach halves and 1 tbsp of the liquid
1 tsp ground cardamom

Method

* The first thing to do is to strain the yoghurt the night before using. Shrikhand is a very thick-set dessert, and all the liquid needs to be drained out of the yoghurt until what's left is thick curds. Transfer yoghurt to a cheesecloth or muslin. Tie up and leave hanging from a tap for at least 2 hours or better yet, overnight.
* To prepare the shrikhand, place the drained yogurt in a large mixing bowl, and sift in the icing sugar.
* Mix well to form a smooth, creamy mixture.
* Fold in the cardamom, pistachios, and the reserved peach juice.
* Roughly chop the peach halves, and divide between 4 serving glasses.
* Pour the yoghurt mixture on top of the peaches.
* Chill for at least 2 hours before serving.

Peach Shrikhand

MANGO AND PASSION FRUIT BHAPA DOI

(Serves 8)

When I first came across this dessert, I was quite surprised to find that there is an Indian equivalent to cheesecake. It just never occurred to me that such a recipe would exist in Indian cuisine. Bhapa doi, which literally means "steamed yogurt," is a Bengali dessert. Traditionally just sweetened and fragranced with the usual cardamom and pistachio, it can be made in a variety of flavours, and the only obvious difference between this and cheesecake is that this doesn't have a biscuit base.

Ingredients
400 g can sweetened condensed milk
200 ml double cream
200 ml thick yoghurt
200 ml mango pulp (fresh or canned)
2 passion fruits

Method
* Heat oven to gas mark 4/180°C/350°F, and grease and line a 15-cm (6") springform cake tin.
* Place the condensed milk, cream, yoghurt, and mango pulp in a large mixing bowl, and whisk together until smooth.
* Pour the mixture into the prepared cake tin, and place the tin inside a large roasting dish.
* Fill the roasting dish with hot water until it reaches half way up the sides of the cake tin.
* Very carefully place the entire roasting dish into the middle of the preheated oven.
* Bake for 30–35 minutes or until firm.
* Once baked, allow to cool on a wire rack. When the water has cooled, remove the cake tin from the roasting dish, and place directly on the rack.
* Transfer the room-temperature cake to the fridge, and leave to chill overnight.
* Run a knife around the edge of the bhapa doi, unclip the cake tin, and gently ease the doi out and onto a serving plate.
* Scoop out the flesh of the passion fruit. Mix with a little sugar to taste if necessary, and spread on top of the doi.
* Cut into slices, and serve chilled.

Mango and Passionfruit Bhapa Doi

AFTER-DINNER DESSERTS
(FUSION)

My fusion recipes combine the flavours of the Indian desserts Mum would treat me to at home, with the desserts I have come to know and love living in London. It's been so fun and exciting to develop these over the years and I hope you enjoy them as much as I do.

COCONUT AND GINGER CHEESECAKE

(Serves 12)

Coconut and ginger is a flavour combination most often attributed to the West Indies and Caribbean, but it's also really common in south India. Coconuts can be found growing in abundance all across south India, and this is reflected in the cuisine which uses lots of coconut milk, fresh and dried coconut, and coconut oil to name a few. This recipe was created for Mum, who loves coconut, and Dad, who loves ginger.

Ingredients

24 ginger biscuits
100 g unsalted butter
200 g cream cheese
150 g icing sugar
1 tsp ground cardamom
200 ml coconut milk
300 ml double cream
5cm stemmed ginger, and 1-tsp stem ginger syrup
fresh grated coconut to garnish

Method

* Grease and line a 20-cm (8") springform cake tin.
* Finely crush the biscuits into a large mixing bowl. Melt the butter, and stir it into the biscuit crumbs making sure all of the crumbs are coated.
* Press the biscuit mixture into the base of the cake tin, and use the back of a spoon to make it as level as possible.
* Refrigerate the biscuit base while preparing the filling.
* Beat the cream cheese until it becomes soft, and then sift in the icing sugar.
* Beat together to combine, and then beat in the cardamom.
* Gently whisk in the coconut milk to form a smooth, thick paste.
* In a separate large bowl, whisk the cream until soft peaks form.
* Add the cream cheese mixture to the cream, and gently fold in to combine.
* Finely chop the stemmed ginger and add to the cream mixture alongside the ginger syrup, and gently swirl it all together.
* Pour the cheesecake mixture into the cake tin, level the surface, and sprinkle generously with the grated coconut.
* Chill overnight for the flavours to mature and the cake to set.
* Cut into slices, and serve chilled.

Coconut And Ginger Cheesecake

POMEGRANATE LIME MOUSSE

(Serves 4)

Pomegranates are hugely popular in India. Their brilliant ruby-red seeds and orange rinds represent the colourful culture of the country and for many; the plentiful seeds inside the fruit represent fertility, prosperity, and grandeur. This light mousse combines pomegranate and lime to create a vibrant, sweet-and-sour, refreshing dessert perfect for summer.

Ingredients

2 pomegranates
50 g caster sugar
250 ml water
1 lime
1 sachet vegetarian gelatine
600 ml double cream
80 g icing sugar
4 tbsp honey, plus extra for garnishing

Method

* Remove the seeds from the pomegranates and discard the rinds.
* Set aside 4 tbsp of the seeds and place the rest in a saucepan with the caster sugar and 50 ml of the water.
* Stew over a medium heat for about 5 minutes until the seeds soften and release their juices.
* Push through a fine sieve so you are left with a thick, seedless pomegranate puree.
* Finely zest the lime. Keep the zest aside, and squeeze the juice into a clean bowl.
* Whisk the vegetarian gelatine into cold water, and then gently bring this water to the boil whisking it continuously.
* Divide the gelatine mixture equally between the lime juice and pomegranate puree.
* Whisk both of the mixtures thoroughly, and leave them aside to cool.
* Keep ready 4 clear glasses to serve the mousse.
* In a large mixing bowl, whisk the cream until soft peaks form.
* Fold the icing sugar and honey into the cream until well combined.
* Divide the mixture into 2 bowls.
* Carefully fold the pomegranate jelly into 1 bowl of cream and the lime jelly into the second bowl of cream making sure both the mixtures are well combined. (The jelly mixtures should still be runny even though they need to have cooled slightly. If they have begun to set, you can reheat them to make them liquid again.)
* Spoon half of the pomegranate mousse into the bases of the four serving glasses, and lightly tap to level them.
* Divide the lime mousse equally between the 4 glasses, carefully layering it on top of the pomegranate mousse.
* Finally divide the second half of the pomegranate mousse between the four desserts.
* Top with the extra pomegranate seeds and an extra drizzle of honey.
* Refrigerate to chill for a few hours, and serve cold.

Pomegranate Lime Mousse

LYCHEE PANNA COTTA

(Makes 4)

Traditionally a classic Italian dessert, panna cotta is made by cooking cream and setting it to produce a wonderfully smooth, dense dessert. Due to the reverence of cows in Indian culture, buffalo milk is widely used and so any rich, milk-based recipe fits perfectly into Indian cuisine. Lychees, one of my favourite fruits, were introduced to India via the Far East and have since become well-loved throughout the country— although they are still considered quite a luxury. Their sweet floral taste is intense, addictive, and perfectly complimented by the ginger in this recipe.

Ingredients

200 g fresh lychees, peeled and de-stoned
2½ tbsp rose water
250 ml double cream
250 ml whole milk
2½ tbsp caster sugar
1½ sachets vegetarian gelatine
1 inch piece of stem ginger
½ tsp stem ginger syrup
200 g strawberries
3 tbsp water

Method

* Start by pureeing the lychees alongside 2 tbsp of the rose water, and then pass the mixture through a sieve, and discard any pulp.
* Combine the cream and milk in a saucepan with the lychee puree and 2 tbsp of sugar.
* Add 1 sachet of the vegetarian gelatine and whisk well.
* Place the pan over a medium heat, and allow the contents to warm through.
* Remove the pan from the heat just before the cream mixture comes to a boil.
* Finely chop the piece of stem ginger, and stir into the cream alongside the ginger syrup.
* Divide the cream mixture between 4 serving bowls and leave to cool.
* While the panna cotta cools, hull the strawberries and puree them with the remaining rose water.
* Strain into a saucepan, and combine with 3 tbsp cold water.
* Add the remaining sugar and gelatine, and whisk well.
* Place the saucepan over a medium heat until just before the mixture boils.
* Allow the jelly to cool slightly, and then divide between the 4 serving bowls, creating a thin layer on top of each panna cotta.(Make sure the panna cotta is firm to the touch before you pour on the jelly.)
* Chill for at least 4 hours or preferably overnight, and serve with fresh strawberries.

Lychee Panna Cotta

SPICED CRÈME CARAMEL

(Makes 4)

Indians are known for their love of spicy food, and my family is no different. This chai-masala enhanced crème caramel provides a difference from the norm with its fragrant spice flavours. The chai masala does alter the smooth texture slightly, but we like the little speckles of cinnamon, clove, cardamom, and ginger as they come through the dense milk base. If you prefer the smoother version, try using a liquid chai extract instead.

Ingredients

250 g caster sugar
3 tbsp water
3 tbsp custard powder
600 ml double cream
2 sachets vegetarian gelatine
2½ tsp chai masala (see page 4)
½ tsp vanilla extract

Method

* Place 150 g of the sugar in a heavy-based pan, shake to level, and sprinkle the water on top.
* Place over a high heat.
* Allow to heat until the edges of the sugar start to change colour, and then give the pan a shake to mix it slightly.
* Return to the heat and allow to melt, giving the pan a shake every few minutes to stop the sugar from burning.
* Continue to cook the caramel, swirling the pan every now and then once the sugar has begun to melt, until you have an evenly coloured, deep golden-brown caramel.
* Working fairly quickly, divide the caramel between 4 individual-sized ramekins, swirling them to coat the base and sides with the caramel. (Take extra care as the caramel will be very hot.)
* Leave aside to cool while you prepare the custard filling.
* Whisk the custard powder into 100 ml of the double cream in a large mixing bowl, and leave aside.
* Pour the rest of the cream into a saucepan, and whisk in the gelatine, the rest of the sugar, chai masala, and vanilla extract.
* Turn on the heat under the cream, and continue whisking until the cream becomes hot.
* Pour the hot cream into the cold cream, whisk to combine, return the entire mixture to the saucepan, and return to the heat.
* Bring the mixture back up to a simmer.
* Divide the mixture between the 4 ramekins. Allow them to rest for about 30 minutes until they feel set to the touch.
* Run a knife around the edge of each ramekin, turn out onto a serving plate, and serve warm or well chilled.

Spiced Creme Caramel

PASSION FRUIT AND ROSE-WATER CRÈME BRÛLÉE

(Makes 4)

Crème brûlée is one of those desserts that most people love, and it is so versatile in that it provides the perfect base for a variety of flavours. While we've enjoyed many chocolate, fruit, and coffee varieties at home and in restaurants, this particular flavour combination seems to be the all-round winner in my family. The tart passion fruit adds a fruity depth to the custard, which is beautifully harmonised by the sweet, floral rose-water topping.

Ingredients
2 tbsp custard powder
50 g caster sugar
2 passion fruit
400 ml whole milk

For topping
4 tbsp rose water
4 tbsp caster sugar

Method
* Preheat oven to gas mark 2/150°C/300°F.
* Place 4 ramekins inside a large roasting pan, and keep aside.
* Combine the custard powder and sugar in a bowl with the pulp (including seeds) from both passion fruit and 50 ml of the milk.
* Whisk well to combine, and leave aside.
* Heat the remaining milk in a saucepan over a medium heat until boiling.
* Carefully pour the boiling milk over the custard-powder mixture.
* Whisk thoroughly until smooth.
* Pass the entire mixture through a sieve to remove the seeds, and pour back into the saucepan.
* Heat gently, whisking continuously until simmering and thick enough to coat the back of a spoon.
* Divide the custard equally between the ramekins.
* Fill the roasting pan with hot water from a kettle until it reaches half way up the sides of the ramekins.
* Place in the oven and bake for about 30 minutes or until the custards are set but slightly wobbly.
* Carefully remove from the oven, and allow to cool slightly before removing the ramekins from the roasting pan.
* Cover the ramekins with plastic wrap, and chill for 4 hours or overnight.
* Sprinkle a tbsp of sugar and rose water on top of each custard and place under a high grill until melted, caramelised and dark brown. (If you have a mini kitchen blow torch, use it.)
* Allow the caramel to cool slightly before serving. (The custard should remain chilled.)

Passion Fruit and Rose-water Creme Brulee

EXOTIC FRUIT PUFFS

(Serves 8)

So many varieties of fresh fruit are so widely available in India that it's exciting to come up with new things to do with them. As much as we love to dry fruit and pickle it, the best way to eat fruit is fresh when it is at its ripest and sweetest. Mum used to make an amazing fruit salad with a bit of coconut and saffron, which went on to inspire this Indian style fruit puff. Use any fresh fruit. It all tastes great with this coconut and saffron custard.

Ingredients

500 g puff pastry
2 tbsp instant custard powder
50 g caster sugar
200 ml whole milk
200 ml coconut milk
½ tsp saffron
¼ tsp ground cardamom
5 tbsp apricot jam
fruit of your choice

Method

* Preheat oven to gas mark 6/200°C/400°F.
* Roll out the pastry on a floured surface until it is around 1-cm thick.
* Cut into 8 x 8 cm squares.
* Carefully score a 1-cm border around the edge of each square. Use a sharp knife and take care not to pierce right through the pastry.
* Brush the border of each square with a little milk. Take care so that the milk does not go over the scored line.
* Bake for 10 minutes or until puffed and golden.
* Transfer to a wire rack to cool completely.
* In the meantime prepare the custard. In a large mixing bowl whisk the custard powder and sugar together with 50 ml of the milk.
* Warm up the rest of the milk and the coconut milk together with the saffron in a saucepan over a medium heat.
* When the milk is hot, carefully pour it over the custard powder, whisk thoroughly to combine, and then transfer back to the saucepan.
* Return to a low heat, whisking continuously until the custard begins to simmer and has visibly thickened (or is thick enough to coat the back of a spoon).
* Pour back into the mixing bowl, stir in the cardamom, and allow to cool completely. (Stir occasionally to prevent a film forming on top.)
* Warm the apricot jam to make it runny, and then press through a strainer to remove any lumps.
* Return to the baked pastry, and press down the middle of each square so that only the border is still puffed, creating a hollow for the filling.
* Brush the base of each pastry case with some apricot jam. This will help to stop the base becoming soggy when the custard is poured.
* Fill each case about three quarters of the way up with the cooled custard.
* Arrange the fruit on the custard as you desire.
* Brush the fruit with the leftover apricot jam to give it sheen.
* Serve chilled.

Exotic Fruit Puffs

PASSION FRUIT AND STRAWBERRY MILLE FEUILLE

(Makes 6)

Passion fruit is one of my favourite Indian flavours. It's so tangy that it practically fizzes on the tongue, and those crunchy little seeds make eating the fruit really fun. Although it is not originally from India (my guess is that it travelled over with the Portuguese from South America), it has become one of the most popular fruits in the country—especially the more common purple variety, which is used in juices and fruit salads. Here I've paired it with a flaky mille-feuille to add to the texture. The white chocolate and strawberries sweeten the tangy flavour.

Ingredients

300 g puff pastry
80 g white chocolate (broken into pieces)
160 ml double cream
2 tbsp caster sugar (plus extra for sprinkling)
1 passion fruit
a few strawberries
icing sugar for garnish

Method

* On a floured surface, roll out the pastry until it makes a rectangle about 28cm x 30cm.
* Transfer the pastry to a baking sheet, sprinkle with sugar, and refrigerate for 30 minutes.
* In the meantime preheat oven to gas mark 6/200°C/400°F.
* Remove the baking sheet from the fridge, and lay a second baking sheet on top of the pastry before placing in the oven.
* Bake for 20 minutes until the pastry is golden.
* Cool completely on a wire rack.
* When the pastry is cold, trim the edges to make sure they are perfectly straight and then cut three equally sized rows across the width of the pastry.
* Cut each row into 5 equal sections, creating 18 equal pieces of pastry. Leave aside.
* Gently melt the white chocolate, and leave aside to cool while you whip the cream.
* Whip the cream until soft peaks form. Fold in the pulp and seeds of the passion fruit, sugar, and white chocolate.
* Chop the strawberries into small, equal pieces.
* To assemble, pipe dots of cream over the surface of 6 of the pastry sections, and place strawberry chunks in between.
* Place a second piece of pastry on top, and repeat the cream and strawberry layer.
* Top each mille-feuille with the last of the pastry sheets, and dust generously with icing sugar.

Strawberry and Passionfruit Millefeuille

SWEET GOL GAPPE

(Makes 20)

Gol gappe or "pani puri" are one of the most popular street foods in India. Made fresh and served hot from the pan along the roadside in many Indian cities, they are crisp little hollow spheres of pastry that are filled with spicy boiled chickpeas, crunchy savoury snacks and then drenched in spiced yoghurt, mint, and tamarind chutneys. They are truly scrumptious. The trick with these bite-sized morsels is to stuff them as full as you can and then devour them in one large mouthful. That way, you get the crunch from the puri, which gives way to the burst of flavours from the pani—without it spilling all over you. Here's my sweet version, but you can use any flavour you like. For something different, try mango cream with passion fruit seeds, or fold some espresso into the cream and top with chocolate-covered coffee beans.

Ingredients

For the Puri (Pastry Cases)

35 g fine semolina
large pinch of salt
small pinch of baking powder
30 ml hot water (not boiling, and from the tap is fine)
2 tbsp plain flour
½ tsp vegetable oil and extra for deep frying

For the Cream Filling

200 ml whipping cream
4 tbsp icing sugar
1 tbsp cocoa
10 strawberries
1 chocolate-covered honeycomb bar, crushed

For the Chocolate Sauce

200 g dark chocolate
20 g butter
20 g golden syrup
150 ml double cream

Method

* Start by making the puri. Place the semolina, salt, and baking powder into a small bowl and cover with the hot water, mixing it a little to ensure all of the semolina gets soaked.
* Allow to rest for 2 minutes before sifting in the plain flour.
* Mix well, kneading the dough for approximately 5 minutes until it begins to feel less sticky.
* Add the ½ tsp of oil and continue to knead for a further 5 minutes until you are left with soft, elastic dough.
* Cover in cling film, and leave to rest in the fridge for 30 minutes.
* Place a pan filled with 6cm of oil over a medium heat to warm. Meanwhile roll the puris. Preheat oven to gas mark 2/150°C/300°F.
* Divide the dough into 2, and roll out one half on a lightly floured surface to about a 2-mm thickness. (Take care when doing this. If the dough is too thick or too thin, it will not rise when fried.)
* Use a 5.5-cm round cutter to cut out circles from the rolled out pastry.
* Fry in the hot oil until puffed and very lightly golden on both sides, and drain on kitchen paper.
* Repeat until you have used up all of the dough.
* After frying, you may find that some of the puris are still a little on the soft side. Place them on a baking tray and into the warm oven for about 20 minutes until hard and crisp.
* Cool on a wire rack.
* While the puris are cooling, prepare the whipped-cream filling. Whip the cream until semi-stiff peaks form.
* Fold in the icing sugar, cocoa, and about half of the crushed chocolate honeycomb.

- Chop the strawberries into small chunks, and keep them refrigerated alongside the cream while preparing the sauce.
- Gently melt the dark chocolate and butter in a microwave or bowl set above a larger bowl of simmering water, stirring occasionally.
- When the chocolate is almost melted but not quite, stir in the golden syrup.
- Melt together, and remove from the heat.
- Allow the mixture to cool slightly before stirring in the double cream.
- To assemble the sweet gol gappe, fill each puri a third of the way up with the chocolate-cream mixture, top with a generous amount of strawberry chunks, and top with more cream until it oozes out from the top.
- Spoon lots of chocolate sauce over each stuffed puri, and sprinkle with more chocolate honeycomb, and any extra strawberry chunks.
- Serve immediately.

Sweet Gol Gappe

EXOTIC FRUIT TRIFLE

(Serves 8)

When my parents and their siblings came to England in the late sixties and early seventies, the trifle was going through a bit of a revival. Versions included jelly and whipped cream, and were then dressed with glace cherries, ingredients my parents were not so familiar with in Africa. They were amazed. I think they've been in love with trifles ever since. My version represents the fruits of India with mangoes, passion fruit, coconut, and lychees. Delicious!

Ingredients

425g tinned lychees
200 ml lychee juice
1 tbsp rose water
1 sachet vegetarian gelatine
pink food colouring if desired
1 egg free sponge cake (page 5)
250 ml passion fruit juice
2 tbsp instant custard powder
400 ml whole milk
200 ml strained mango pulp (about 2
 mangoes worth or use tinned)
300 ml whipping cream
60 g icing sugar
100 ml coconut cream
1 passion fruit
toasted flaked almonds to garnish
caster sugar for sprinkling

Method

* Begin by preparing an egg free sponge cake as directed on page 5.
* To make the jelly, drain the tinned lychees, reserving the juice in a saucepan. (It should be around 200 ml.)
* Roughly chop 100 g of the drained lychees and place in the bottom of a serving bowl.
* Top up the syrup from the lychees with the extra lychee juice and rose water so that you have 400 ml altogether in the saucepan.
* Mix well and taste. You may find you need to add a little sugar.
* Whisk in the vegetarian gelatine, and place the saucepan over a gentle heat.
* Allow the liquid to come to the boil, and then switch off the heat and allow to cool slightly.
* Stir in a drop or two of pink food colouring if desired, and then pour the jelly mixture over the lychees, and leave to cool.
* Slice the cake horizontally so that you have a layer approximately 2-cm in height.
* Roughly cut the cake so that it will fit in one layer on top of the jelly in the serving bowl.
* Soak the sponge in the passion fruit juice for about 2 seconds on each side, and then gently place on top of the lukewarm jelly. (It will sink slightly into the jelly and then just come to rest above the surface.)
* To prepare the custard, whisk the custard powder with about 50 ml of the milk in a large mixing bowl and leave aside.
* Heat up the rest of the milk until boiling and then carefully whisk into the custard-powder mixture to combine.
* Return the mixture to the saucepan, and heat the custard over a low heat, whisking continuously until simmering and visibly thickened (enough to coat the back of a spoon).
* Transfer back to the mixing bowl, sweeten to taste, and allow to cool slightly.
* When the mixture is lukewarm, stir in the mango pulp, and pour the custard over the sponge in the trifle.

* Level the surface with the back of a spoon or palette knife and refrigerate.
* Allow the custard to cool completely before preparing the cream.
* Whip the cream until soft peaks form, and then fold in the icing sugar and coconut cream.
* Pour the cream over the trifle.
* Garnish with the pulp from the passion fruit, toasted flaked almonds, and a sprinkling of caster sugar.
* Chill for at least 4 hours or overnight.

Exotic Fruit Trifle

COFFEE MASALA TIRAMISU

(Serves 8)

The Italian dessert, tiramisu, is renowned for its rich coffee flavour and layers of fluffy cream and soft sponge. These days you often find tiramisu served with chocolate folded into the recipe. There are so many variations that each person can have his or her own favourite. This spiced version reminds me of the tiny little cups of espresso generously blended with chai masala that Jay discovered on his most recent trip to India.

Ingredients

1 egg-free sponge cake (page 5)
150 ml boiling water
2 tsp instant coffee granules
3 tsp chai masala (page 4)
300 ml whipping cream
40 g icing sugar
20 g cocoa

Method

* Start by making the egg-free sponge cake as directed on page 5. Once baked, leave it to cool on a wire rack.
* Dissolve the coffee granules in the boiling water and stir in 1½ tsp of the chai masala. Allow the mixture to cool.
* To prepare the cream, whip until soft peaks form; and then fold in the sugar, cocoa, and the remaining chai masala. Keep refrigerated until needed.
* When the cake is completely cool, carefully slice off the domed top and discard.
* Carefully slice the levelled cake into two equal layers.
* Starting with the bottom layer of the cake, dip it into the espresso mixture. Allow to soak for 1 second, then flip and soak the other side before placing carefully onto a serving plate.
* Top with half of the cream mixture.
* Repeat until you have used up all of the cake and cream.
* Sprinkle with a little more icing sugar and cocoa if desired, and then refrigerate overnight.
* Serve chilled.

Coffee Masala Tiramisu

MANGO FOOL

(Makes 4)

Here's a slightly different take on the customary mango lassi. A traditional drink made using yoghurt; lassi comes in many different sweet and savoury varieties, and is very similar to a smoothie. My parents always have the savoury version alongside their lunch on hot, summer days; but the sweet version has always been my favourite. This recipe is a bit more substantial than a lassi. It falls somewhere between fruit yoghurt and a milkshake. It's an ideal light, summer pudding.

Ingredients

2 ripe alphonso mangoes
200 ml double cream
1 tsp vanilla extract
40 g icing sugar
150 g natural yoghurt

Method

* Peel and chop the mangoes into to 1-cm cubes.
* Place about a tbsp of mango chunks in the bottom of each glass, and puree the rest.
* Whip the cream until it reaches a soft-peak consistency.
* Fold in the vanilla extract, icing sugar, and yogurt.
* Combine half of the whipped-cream mixture with half of the pureed mango.
* Split the plain whipped-cream mixture between the 4 glasses, and then follow with the mango puree.
* Lastly, top each glass with the mango whipped-cream mixture.
* Garnish with a mint leaf if desired, and serve chilled.

Mango Fool

DRINKS AND FROZEN DESSERTS

Trying to keep cool during hot Indian summers can be tricky, but putting your feet up and relaxing in the afternoon warmth with a cool, refreshing, delicious drink or dessert can be just the trick. This selection of recipes is perfect for the summer time. Think barbecues and garden picnics.

MANGO AND CARDAMOM LASSI

(Serves 5)

Here's a classic lassi recipe. When I was young I used to love this drink so much that I think I put my family off it. I made it weekend after weekend for the whole summer, every year. Although I don't make it as often anymore, I still love it, and I think my family have rekindled their taste for it too.

Ingredients
2 large alphonso mangoes or 400 ml alphonso mango pulp
1 tsp ground cardamom
400 ml plain yoghurt
200 ml milk

Method
* Peel the mangoes and remove the stone. Place the flesh in a large mixing bowl, and blend into a puree; or simply pour mango pulp into a mixing bowl, and whisk to make it slightly frothy.
* Blend in the yoghurt, adding more or less until the lassi is to the desired consistency.
* Whisk in the cardamom, and add a little sugar to taste.
* Serve chilled.

Mango and Cardamom Lassi

BASUNDI

(Serves 2)

This timeless sweet drink can be served hot or chilled at any time of day, night, or year. When we were little, I remember Mum making it for us as a weekend treat, and I still love it. There are many variations of this recipe, with added fruits, nuts, even chocolate; but here is the recipe I know and love the best.

Ingredients

1 L whole milk
pinch of saffron threads
2 tbsp coarsely ground pistachios
2 tbsp coarsely chopped almonds
100 g caster sugar
½ tsp ground cardamom
pinch of nutmeg if desired

Method

* Place the milk in a large heavy-based saucepan over a medium heat.
* Allow the milk to warm through, and then stirring continuously so that the milk doesn't stick to the pan, cook the milk until it reduces by one third.
* The reduction process will take quite a while, but don't be tempted to turn up the heat, as this will make the milk stick to the pan and the finished basundi will have lumps in it. Be prepared to stand and stir diligently for up to 45 minutes.
* Stir in the saffron, nuts, and sugar and cook for a further 15 minutes
* Turn off the heat, stir in the cardamom, and divide between 4 serving cups
* Basundi can be served hot. Alternatively chill in the fridge overnight for a dense milky dessert. If doing this, allow the milk to come to room temperature, stirring every now and then so it doesn't form a skin on top, and then transfer to cups before refrigerating.

Basundi

ICED CHAI LATTE

(Makes 1)

Don't get me wrong. I love masala chai, but on a gloriously warm summer's day it just isn't what I need in terms of a pick-me-up. Solution? Iced chai latte. It's cold and refreshing with invigorating spice. This equivalent to a hot cup of chai will happily see you through the summer and perhaps even into the winter. I think my homemade version is far better than those available in many coffee shops today.

Ingredients
1 tsp black tea
½ tsp chai masala (page 4)
1 tsp sugar
50 ml water
150 ml milk
1 scoop vanilla ice cream
lots of ice to serve

Method
* Place the tea, chai masala, and sugar in a pan with the water and milk. Bring to a boil.
* Reduce the heat and allow to simmer for 2 minutes.
* Strain the masala chai into a cup, and allow to cool to room temperature. Then refrigerate for a few hours to become nice and cold.
* When chilled, pour the tea into a blender.
* Add the scoop of ice cream and an ice cube.
* Blend until smooth.
* Pour into a tall glass filled with ice, and enjoy.

Iced Chai Latte

ROSE AND VANILLA KULFI

Kulfi is the Indian version of ice cream. Originating from the north of India, it was traditionally made from fresh bull's milk, which is thicker than cow's milk. The milk would be sweetened and then boiled over a low heat for hours until it reduced down to less than a quarter of its original volume. The thickened, sweet milk would then be transferred into small clay pots, which would be wrapped in masses of snow collected from the Himalayan Mountains to freeze it before it could be served to only the most distinguished VIPs. My recipe is far easier. Minimum effort required for what is still such a regal dessert.

Ingredients

200 ml whole milk
2 tbsp corn flour
398 g tin sweetened condensed milk
400 ml double cream
400 ml evaporated milk
75 ml rose water
1 vanilla pod
½ tsp vanilla extract (optional)
a few drops of pink food colouring (optional)

Method

* Pour the whole milk into a small saucepan, and whisk in the corn flour.
* Warm over a low heat, and continue whisking until the corn flour has dissolved into the milk to thicken it. It should take no more than 5 minutes.
* Remove from the heat, and leave aside to cool.
* Combine the condensed milk, double cream, and evaporated milk in a large mixing bowl.
* Whisk until well combined, thick, and foamy.
* Add the cooled whole milk and rose water, and scrape out the seeds from the vanilla pod, and add those too.
* Whisk together, and make sure all of the ingredients are really well combined.
* At this stage, taste the mixture; and if you feel you need to, add in the vanilla extract to intensify the flavour.
* Mix in the pink food colouring if desired to produce a thick rose-coloured custard.
* Pour the mixture either into individual freezer-proof moulds or a 1.5 L ice cream container, and freeze overnight.
* The kulfi will be quite hard when it comes out of the freezer, so to serve, remove from the freezer about 15 minutes in advance.

Rose and Vanilla Kulfi

SAFFRON AND CARDAMOM ICE CREAM

Traditionally in India, desserts were considered a luxury and would only be served on extra special occasions or to royalty, which is also why they would contain such expensive and rare ingredients. Today saffron and cardamom are more widely available, but this ice cream still tastes incredibly rich and exotic. It's perfect for those special occasions when you want to serve something indulgent yet informal.

Ingredients

1 L whole milk
¼ tsp saffron threads
100 g milk powder
150 g caster sugar
500 ml double cream
1 tsp ground cardamom

Method

* Place the whole milk in a heavy-based saucepan over a high heat.
* When the milk has warmed, stir in the saffron and continue to heat until the milk comes to a boil.
* Reduce the heat slightly, and simmer until the milk has reduced by a quarter, around 15–20 minutes
* Turn off the heat, cover, and leave to rest for about 10 minutes so that the flavour of the saffron can mature.
* Return the pan to a low heat, and sift in the milk powder and sugar.
* Stir continuously until the sugar dissolves and the milk is just starting to simmer.
* Turn off the heat, stir in the double cream and cardamom, and allow the mixture to cool to room temperature. (Give it a stir every now and then to make sure a skin doesn't form on top.)
* Refrigerate the ice-cream mixture overnight.
* Freeze in an ice-cream maker following the manufacturer's directions.
* Transfer to a 2-L ice-cream container, and store in the freezer; or for best results, serve immediately.

Saffron and Cardamom Ice Cream

ICE-CREAM SUNDAE À LA INDIA

(Makes 4)

There are so many individual ingredients that spring to mind when you think of India, especially when it comes to fruit and desserts. There are some ingredients however that stand out more than others; such as mango the national fruit of India, sweetened milk dishes, saffron and cardamom. This ice-cream sundae is quick and easy to make, is an instant taste of India with all these key flavours combined, looks gorgeous, and is a great way to use the saffron and cardamom ice-cream recipe, found on page 112.

Ingredients

100 g caster sugar
250 ml water
pinch of saffron threads
saffron and cardamom ice cream (recipe on page 159 or for a quick fix just fold some cardamom into softened store-bought vanilla ice cream)
2 Indian mangoes
2 passion fruits
1 pomegranate
20 green grapes
100 g roasted plain pistachios
100 g flaked almonds
aerated whipped cream to top each sundae

Method

* Place the sugar and water in a heavy-based saucepan over a medium heat.
* Allow to heat through just until the sugar dissolves and it thickens slightly. (Heat no more than 5 minutes. The mixture should remain clear.)
* Turn off the heat, stir in the saffron, and leave aside to cool.
* Remove the ice cream from the freezer to thaw while you prepare the fruit.
* Peel the mangoes and chop into 1-cm cubes.
* Cut the passion fruits in half, scoop out the flesh, and place on top of the mangoes.
* De-seed the pomegranate and place the fruit in with the mango and passion fruit.
* Cut the grapes in half, add to the rest of the fruit, and gently toss it all together to combine.
* Place 2 tsp of the fruit mixture into the bottom of a tall sundae glass.
* Top with a scoop of ice cream, and drizzle with the sugar syrup.
* Sprinkle some of the nuts on top of the ice cream, and continue to layer fruit, ice cream syrup, and nuts as you desire until you reach the top of the glass The top layer should be fruit.
* Swirl on a generous amount of whipped cream, drizzle over any remaining sugar syrup, and place a pomegranate seed at the top for good measure.

Ice-Cream Sundae à la India

WATERMELON AND STRAWBERRY SPICE SORBET

As a child I would be completely baffled to see the grown-ups in my family attack large slices of mango and watermelon with ground ginger and chilli. Despite all their efforts to make me understand how the spices cut through the sweetness of the fruit to produce an intense, tingly, sweet, sour, and spicy experience on the tongue; I thought they were completely insane. Now however, I completely get it. Combining sweet and savoury does indeed work and tastes amazing. Try it!

Ingredients

1 kg watermelon flesh (seedless or deseeded)
2 limes
300 g strawberries (hulled)
60 g caster sugar
1½ tsp ginger (peeled and grated)
2 tsp chilli flakes

Method

* Chop the watermelon and strawberries into chunks, and place in a large mixing bowl.
* Add the juice from the limes alongside the sugar and ginger, and mix well.
* Cover with cling film, and allow to rest in the fridge for no more than 1 hour.
* Pour the contents of the bowl into a blender, and pulse to create a smooth puree.
* Pass the mixture through a sieve into the bowl of an ice cream maker, and freeze according to the manufacturer's instructions.
* Just before the sorbet is set, add the chilli flakes so they can be folded in during the last minute or two of the freezing process.
* Serve immediately, garnished with a sprig of fresh mint; or transfer to an ice-cream container and freeze. Remove from the freezer 15 minutes before serving to make it easier to scoop.
* If you do not have an ice-cream maker, pour the puree into a container and freeze as normal.
* Break up the sorbet using a fork every hour until it has set completely; fold in the chilli flakes when the sorbet is almost firm.

Watermelon and Strawberry Spiced Sorbet

CONVERSION CHART

FLOUR AND ICING SUGAR

Grams	Cups	Ounces
30 g	¼ C	1 oz.
45 g	1/3 C	1.5 oz.
65 g	½ C	2.25 oz.
85 g	2/3 C	3 oz.
95 g	¾ C	3.5 oz.
130 g	1 C	4.5 oz.

GRANULATED SUGAR

Grams	Cups	Ounces
50 g	¼ Cup	1.75 oz.
70 g	1/3 Cup	2.5 oz.
100 g	½ Cup	3.5 oz.
135 g	2/3 Cup	4.75 oz.
150 g	¾ Cup	5.5 oz.
200 g	1 Cup	7 oz.

BUTTER

Grams	Cups	Ounces
60 g	¼ Cup	2 oz.
75 g	1/3 Cup	2.6 oz.
112 g	½ Cup	4 oz.
150 g	2/3 Cup	5.5 oz.
170 g	¾ Cup	6 oz.
225 g	1 Cup	8 oz.

WATER

Millilitres	Cups	Fluid Ounces
60 ml	¼ Cup	2 oz.
80 ml	1/3 Cup	3 oz.
125 ml	½ Cup	4 oz.
160 ml	2/3 Cup	5.5 oz.
175 ml	¾ Cup	6 oz.
250 ml	1 Cup	8.5 oz.

INDEX

Printed in Great Britain
by Amazon.co.uk, Ltd.,
Marston Gate.